Cool
Science Jobs

Mary Kay Carson

SCHOLASTIC INC.

New York   Toronto   London   Auckland   Sydney
Mexico City   New Delhi   Hong Kong   Buenos Aires

Cover Photo
© The RoboCup Federation, insert: PhotoDisc via SODA

Copyright © 2003 by Scholastic Inc.
All rights reserved. Published by Scholastic Inc.
Printed in the U.S.A.

ISBN 0-439-59773-0

SCHOLASTIC, SCHOLASTIC ACTION, and associated logos and designs are trademarks and/or registered trademarks of Scholastic Inc.

LEXILE is a registered trademark of MetaMetrics, Inc.

16 15 14 13 12 11   40   12 11 10

Contents

Welcome to This Book

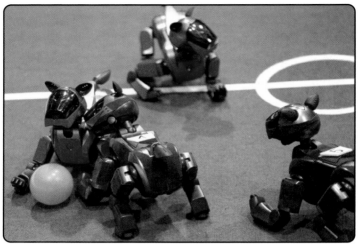

© The RoboCup Federation

What kind of job do you want to have one day? Do you want a job that's fun? Do you want a job that's exciting? Do you want to be a scientist? A scientist? Yes, a scientist!

The scientists in this book have cool jobs. One walks in space. Another teaches soccer to robots. And one scientist rides to the bottom of the ocean in a submarine. Sounds more like fun than work, right? The scientists think so, too.

Read on to learn more about these cool science jobs.

Target Words These words will help you understand these cool science jobs.

- **astronaut** someone who travels to space
  Have you ever wanted to be an astronaut?
- **data** the information that scientists collect
  One scientist gets data from the ocean floor.
- **robot** a machine with movable parts that is controlled by a computer and does jobs often done by a person
  Maybe someday they'll invent a robot that does homework!

Reader Tips Here's how to get the most from this book.

- **Photos** Review the photos that are in this book. Look at the people. What can you tell about them from looking at their photos? What do the photos tell you about their jobs?
- **Draw Conclusions** You can use the photos, chapter heads, captions, and teasers to help you think about the story and to draw conclusions.

1

Take a Hike...in Space

How would you like to take a walk in space?

Bob Curbeam was floating 200 miles above Earth. A cloud of white **crystals** suddenly sped by. He knew the crystals meant trouble.

The crystals were actually a frozen chemical. This chemical is used to cool parts of the **space station.** And it's a deadly poison.

Curbeam and fellow **astronaut** Tom Jones were spacewalking. Both were in spacesuits. They were working outside the space station. They were tied to it with safety cables.

The space station circles Earth out in space. But it isn't a ship. It's more like a building. It was put together in space. Astronauts go up there to do experiments. They want to learn how space affects different plants and animals.

Here, astronaunt Robert Curbeam was getting ready to take his space walk.

Curbeam's friends call him "Beamer." He has spent nearly 20 hours spacewalking.

Houston, We've Got a Problem

Mission controllers in Houston, Texas could see the spacewalkers. Cameras sent video images down to Earth. So everyone at Mission Control saw the crystals float by Curbeam. It worried them, too.

The spacewalkers were safe for now. Their spacesuits protected them. But what would happen when they went back inside the space station? If any crystals were stuck to Curbeam's spacesuit, they could poison the air. Mission controllers asked Curbeam to check his suit carefully.

Chemical Clean-Up

"I can't see anything," said Curbeam. "But I know it sprayed this way." Finding tiny spots on a white suit isn't easy. Doing so while floating in space is even harder.

Heads Up!

What do you think will happen next? Will Curbeam get all the crystals off his suit?

Even a small amount of the chemical could kill them. Luckily, Jones and Curbeam had a brush with them. The mission controllers asked Jones to brush off Curbeam's spacesuit.

Next, Curbeam lay outside in the sunlight for a half-hour. The strong sunlight would bake away any leftover chemical crystals.

Finally, the spacewalkers went inside. They were very careful. They stayed in the **air lock** longer than usual. The air inside the air lock was changed twice. It worked. Whew!

Not Done Yet...

It had been Curbeam's first space walk. And it was a long one. Curbeam and Jones were outside for seven and a half hours. But they wouldn't get much time to rest. Curbeam had two more space walks to do.

Curbeam was part of the *Atlantis* crew on this mission. Space shuttle *Atlantis* had arrived at the space station a few days before. (A space shuttle is kind of like an airplane, only it flies in space.)

Atlantis brought supplies for the space station crew. And it delivered a science lab.

The science lab is called *Destiny*. It is where the scientists grow plants and crystals and do other experiments.

A giant robotic arm hooked up *Destiny* to the station. But lots of hoses and cables had to be connected outside by hand. This was what Curbeam and Jones were doing. One of the hoses started to leak the chemical crystals.

Dreams of Spacewalking

Curbeam used to be a Navy pilot. Then he met Kathy Thornton of **NASA.** Thornton had just returned from a shuttle mission. She told Curbeam about her space walks. She told him what it was like to see the Earth from so far away. And she told him about floating free in space.

"I decided right then and there," said Curbeam. "This is something I want to do."

Heads Up!

Would you want to go for a spacewalk? Do you think it would be exciting or scary? Why?

Curbeam had caught the spacewalking bug! He applied to NASA. Curbeam had worked as an engineer and a **test pilot.** The astronaut program accepted him.

Curbeam had always been interested in space flight. As a kid, he built and flew model airplanes and rockets. "I just loved science," says Curbeam. "I thought the space program was just the most exciting thing."

But he never thought about being an astronaut. He'd always planned on making rockets. "I never thought that I would be the person climbing in," said Curbeam.

Practice Makes Perfect

Curbeam trained one and a half years for the *Atlantis* flight. He practiced every part of the mission. He practiced flying with a fake shuttle. He even practiced spacewalking.

Where can you practice spacewalking on Earth? How about a deep underwater pool? NASA has one that's 40 feet deep. NASA has a full-sized model space station at the bottom of the deep pool. Astronauts put on spacesuits and dive in! It's not easy. The spacesuits weigh 300 pounds. Of course, the suits don't feel as heavy under water.

Down there, they practice connecting hoses. They turn bolts. And they practice all the other tasks they will have to do in space.

Astronauts have fun, too. Curbeam was in a movie about the space station. And he threw out an opening pitch at a Baltimore Orioles' game. Baltimore is Curbeam's hometown. Curbeam even got to meet the President. The crew of *Atlantis* was invited to the White House.

But to Curbeam, there's nothing better than going for a space walk!

Heads Up!

Do you think Curbeam enjoys his job? Why or why not?

2

Risky Bird Business

*This scientist risks his neck
to help save rare falcons.*

Brian Latta is not in a safe place. He's walking along narrow beams. He's on a bridge over Southern California's Long Beach Harbor. Beneath him is a 200-foot drop down to the water. And it's windy.

"Duck!" shouts Latta to a coworker over the traffic noise and wind. A large angry bird dives at them. Its claws and hooked beak are ready for action! The **falcon** screeches by crying *kak-kak-kak*. Its claws rip a hole in Latta's bag. Then it flies off, for now.

"This female is fearless," says Latta. "She knows why I'm here. She's drawn blood before to defend her chicks."

© Peter Lane Taylor

Watch out! Brian Latta climbed out to the nest as the mother falcon dove at him.

Unwelcome Help

Latta opens the ripped bag. He takes out ropes and harnesses. He puts them together.

Latta is a **biologist** who studies falcons. He's here to find the falcon's nest and capture her chicks. The chicks are in danger here. His job is to move them to a safer place.

Peregrine falcons normally build nests on high cliff ledges. But when people start taking over wild places, the birds **adapt.** Peregrines build their nests on skyscrapers, bridges, or radio towers instead. But these aren't safe homes for young chicks.

Dangerous Homes

The young falcons will soon try to fly. Flying takes lots of practice. The chicks will hop and flap. Many will fall into the water below or onto the roadway.

—**Heads Up!**—
Look up adapt *in the glossary. Think of another example of animals having to adapt.*

Workers give Latta a call when they spot nests in dangerous places. Then Latta loads up his climbing gear and heads out. He tries to move as many chicks as possible. "Most would die," says Latta, "if we didn't do this."

Peregrine falcons are rare birds. They nearly died out in the U.S. during the 1970s. **Pollution** makes their eggshells thin. The eggs then break easily. Latta collects eggshells, too. He tests the eggshells for pollution damage. He wants to see if the problem is getting better or worse.

Today there are more peregrine falcons. But they are still rare. Latta cares about each one.

Check Plus

Latta has made nearly 300 climbs. Before every climb, he checks his gear carefully. If he gets knocked off the bridge, he'll fall into empty air. His safety ropes should catch him after about 30 feet. Gulp! Latta says that he still gets scared before each climb.

Latta slowly makes his way toward the nest. There's only one chick. It sees Latta and lets out a loud cry. Latta stops.

It's too late. The mother comes back.

Latta wears a helmet. He raises his arms to protect himself. "Where is she?" Latta shouts. She's heading right for Latta, claws first. The mother strikes his helmet.

Latta sways but doesn't fall. He sits down on the beam. Then he moves forward.

Beware of Mother Falcon

Latta makes it to the nest. Soft white feathers cover the chick. It keeps crying. Latta gets out his chick carrier. Then he gently puts the chick in it. He also grabs some eggshells. He puts them in a plastic bag. The mother comes back as he finishes. She dives at Latta's back but misses. He's okay.

Latta makes his way down. Then he takes a closer look at the chick. It's a three-week-old healthy boy. The chick will be taken to a wild area. Experts will raise it in a safer place. Then the bird will be set free.

All this to save one bird. Latta thinks it's worth it.

3

Journey to the Bottom of the Sea

What secrets lie at the bottom of the sea?

Carol Hirozawa Reiss is looking out the window. All she sees is dark water. "The *Turtle* is taking us down to the ocean floor," she explains. "It's over a mile down. The trip down takes about an hour or more."

The *Turtle* is a special **submarine**. It can dive down very deep. The *Turtle* has cameras, robotic arms, and science tools. It is like a spaceship that works underwater.

Inside the sub, there is little room. It is like being inside a small closet. The lights from the equipment blink like the stars at night.

The sub is diving off the coast of Oregon. Reiss focuses on her work inside the sub.

Carol Hirozawa Reiss is getting into the *Turtle*. It's a small submarine. But it weighs 21 tons!

The *Turtle* finally reaches the ocean floor. Reiss looks for rocks out the window. She takes notes about what she sees. She also records the time of each sighting. She takes her time looking and taking notes. Her **data** must be exact.

Back on land, Reiss will use this data to make a map of the ocean floor. She is studying the rate at which the ocean floor is spreading. She checks instruments that measure the changes every day. The constantly-moving currents make it a hard job.

Hooked on Rocks

Reiss studies rocks and **minerals.** "I love my job," says Reiss. "Everything I do here is interesting to me."

Diving down to the ocean floor seems scary. It is like dropping into a dark, black world. Reiss may be small, but she has lots of courage and loves to try new things. She's also a pilot, scuba diver, and rock climber.

"I didn't know any scientists growing up," says Reiss. "I didn't think I would become a scientist." Then she took a college class called Understanding the Earth. The class hooked Reiss on **geology**! Suddenly Reiss could not learn enough about rocks. She studied them all the time. To Reiss, rocks were like the pages of a book. The layers and layers of rocks told the story of the earth. Reiss says that each rock tells a story.

Heads Up!

How is Reiss's job similar to and different from Curbeam's job?

4

Robot Soccer Champs

These soccer players aren't people—they're robots!

It's a close match. The Berlin team has a deadly kick. Its players send the ball toward the goal with lightning speed! But the Cornell players block it. They have a better plan. Which team will win?

Then the players move through the midfield. They close in around Berlin's goal. A Cornell player gets a shot off! Berlin's goalie moves to block. But the ball sneaks by. Goal!

The crowd jumps to its feet. People cheer and shout. But the players don't move an inch. They stand lifeless on the field. That's because the players aren't alive. They're **robots**! This is RoboCup. It's a yearly soccer competition between teams of robots.

Manuela Veloso's team takes to the field. Go, robots!

Robots That Work Together

Manuela Veloso is in the crowd. She's a computer scientist. A number of her teams play each year at RoboCup. Veloso's team won first place in the RoboCup 2002. Her team competed in the legged **league.** That's the league for robots with four legs. They look like toy dogs. There are also wheeled robot leagues. And there's a **humanoid** robot league. They're shaped like small humans.

Soccer-playing robots have come a long way. "Years ago they could hardly see the ball," says Veloso. "They'd just wander around the field looking lost."

But now the robots kick and block. They run and shoot. And most important, they work together as a team. This is what's interesting to Veloso. She wants to build and program robots that work together.

---**Heads Up!**---
How have soccer-playing robots changed?
What could they do before? And now?

Robots do many jobs already. Some help build cars. Others travel in space. But these robots don't work together. Robot teams could do many jobs better than lone robots. Think of a team of robots going into an earthquake area. They could work together to find victims fast.

From Math to Robots

"I liked math when I was a kid," says Veloso. So she became a computer scientist. "I wanted to make computers **intelligent.**" Intelligent computers can remember things. They can learn from what's happened. They can even make their own decisions.

Scientists program the soccer robot to kick the ball into the goal. Then they watch and see. Does the robot score? What if there are blockers? The computer scientists keep thinking of ways to make the program better.

Heads Up!

Is teaching robots to play soccer just a fun game? Why or why not?

Soccer Makes Robots Smart

Veloso wanted to build smart robots. And having those robots play soccer is a great way to test how smart they are. Soccer is a game with simple rules. But the game plan can be hard. And players must work as a team to win.

Once Veloso and her students program the robots, the robots are on their own. Nobody gives them any more directions. The robots decide on the game plans. They must work together to win.

What's next? "We actually are trying to get to a point where we can play with humans," says Veloso. RoboCup's goal is to have a team of humanoid robots play the winners of the Soccer World Cup of 2050.

On the Watch for Killer Waves

This ocean scientist tracks killer waves.

Villagers felt the ground shake that day in 1988. But earthquakes are common in Papua New Guinea. So, no one gave it too much thought.

The village was gone ten minutes later. It wasn't an earthquake. A giant wave washed the village away. The killer wave was taller than a three-story building. And it was more than two miles long.

The huge wave plowed onto the shore. It crushed everything in its path. Then it pulled back out to sea. It swept away 2,500 people.

Then another killer wave roared in. And then a third wave hit. Finally the giant waves stopped. All that they left behind were a few coconut trees.

Underwater Shake-Ups

These weren't regular ocean waves. "It is a special type of wave," explains ocean scientist Frank González. It's called a **tsunami.**

Tsunamis are caused by underwater earthquakes. "An earthquake pushes the ocean floor up," says González. That means that the water above the ocean floor is shoved up, too. This creates a giant wave.

"It's like when you're getting into the tub," says González.

What happens if you get in carefully? You don't make a mess. What happens if you jump in? "You cause big waves," explains González.

Do the Math

Frank González knows a lot about tsunamis. He studied them nearly every day for many years. González has seen what they can do. He's visited tsunami sites all over the world.

How did González become an ocean scientist? González, who is from Texas, says he loved animals as a kid. "I caught my share of snakes, horned toads, and spiders." But he never saw a live ocean creature until he went **snorkeling.** "I was amazed by the sea life I saw."

Why did González become a tsunami expert? "My love of mathematics," says González. He uses math to describe what happens when a tsunami hits a coast.

On Tsunami Watch

The plan is to track tsunamis at sea—before they hit land. "The system is made up of six deep-ocean stations," says González. These stations will report any tsunamis. And they keep track of where they're headed.

The places in the tsunami's path can then be warned. People will have time to get away. This would save many lives. It could help stop what happened in Papua New Guinea.

Heads Up!

Tsunamis are sometimes called tidal waves. But actually, they don't have anything to do with tides!

James Anderson/NOAA

Frank González is an ocean scientist and tsunami expert.

Glossary

adapt *(verb)* to change because you are in a new situation (p. 15)

air lock *(noun)* an airtight room (p. 9)

astronaut *(noun)* someone who travels to space (p. 6)

biologist *(noun)* someone who studies living things (p. 15)

crystal *(noun)* a clear, ice-like substance (p. 6)

data *(noun)* the information that scientists collect (p. 19)

falcon *(noun)* a fast-flying hawk (p. 13)

geology *(noun)* the science of the earth (p. 20)

humanoid *(adjective)* looking like a human being (p. 23)

intelligent *(adjective)* able to understand, think, and learn (p. 24)

league *(noun)* a group of teams that compete against each other (p. 23)

minerals *(noun)* the solid elements that make up rocks (p. 20)

NASA *(noun)* the National Aeronautics and Space Administration. It's the U.S. government's space agency. (p. 10)

pollution *(noun)* harmful materials that hurt the air, water, and soil (p. 16)

robot *(noun)* a machine with movable parts that is controlled by a computer and does jobs often done by a person (p. 21)

snorkel *(verb)* to swim underwater by breathing through a tube (p. 28)

space station *(noun)* a spacecraft large enough to house a crew for long periods of time (p. 6)

submarine *(noun)* a ship that can travel both on the surface and under water (p. 18)

test pilot *(noun)* a pilot who flies new airplanes to see how they perform (p. 11)

tsunami *(noun)* a giant ocean wave, or tidal wave (p. 27)

Index